SOARING IN STYLE

How Amelia Earhart Became a Fashion Icon

by Jennifer Lane Wilson

illustrated by Lissy Marlin

CAPSTONE EDITIONS
a capstone imprint

Published by Capstone Editions, an imprint of Capstone.
1710 Roe Crest Drive
North Mankato, Minnesota 56003
capstonepub.com

Library of Congress Cataloging-in-Publication Data
Names: Wilson, Jennifer Lane, 1971–2020, author.
Title: Soaring in style : how Amelia Earhart became a fashion icon / by Jennifer Lane Wilson.
Description: North Mankato, Minnesota : Capstone Editions, an imprint of Capstone, [2022] | Includes bibliographical references. | Audience: Ages 8–10. | Audience: Grades 4–6. | Summary: "Long before Amelia Earhart became a superstar, she was a girl who longed to touch the stars. But the dresses women had to wear at the time made those dreams seem almost impossible. Amelia didn't let that stop her. As a young aviator breaking records and expectations, she learned to fly her plane with flair. Later, she dared to create a trendsetting fashion line for active women like herself. *Soaring in Style* tells the groundbreaking story of how Amelia Earhart defied expectations in the air and on the ground to become America's first celebrity fashion designer."—Provided by publisher.
Identifiers: LCCN 2021015978 (print) | LCCN 2021015979 (ebook) | ISBN 9781684464289 (hardcover) | ISBN 9781684464531 (pdf) | ISBN 9781684464555 (kindle edition)
Subjects: LCSH: Earhart, Amelia, 1897–1937—Influence—Juvenile literature. | Air pilots—United States—Biography—Juvenile literature. | Women air pilots—United States—Biography—Juvenile literature. | Fashion designers—United States—Biography—Juvenile literature.
Classification: LCC TL540.E3 W554 2022 (print) | LCC TL540.E3 (ebook) | DDC 629.13092 [B]—dc23
LC record available at https://lccn.loc.gov/2021015978
LC ebook record available at https://lccn.loc.gov/2021015979

Designed by Kay Fraser

Printed and bound in the China.   4545

For the adventurers, adrenaline junkies, and athletes,
like my daughter, who also adores fashion,
and for my family, who are my very own bluest of skies
–JLW

In Kansas, where there are no mountains or oceans, the sky is the most beautiful thing for miles. Long before she became a famous aviator, young Amelia Earhart wanted to touch that beckoning blue and wrap it around her like a cape.

In those days, though, girls had to wear dresses everywhere. That made reaching the sky seem almost impossible.

Amelia lived in a small town with her grandmother and grandfather.
They were stern and sensible. They expected Amelia to keep her feet
on the ground.

But she longed to be up in the air. . . .

Like most girls in the early 1900s who had to wear dresses everywhere, Amelia learned to sew her own clothes. She made clothes for her dolls too.

But busy Amelia didn't like to sit for too long. Amelia wanted to *fly*!

But how to fly with no plane? A roller coaster! With help from her friends and little sister, Amelia built one.

Amelia took the first ride—and the first *CRASH*.

"It's just like flying!" she exclaimed.

Amelia couldn't stop smiling. But she knew she needed better clothes for her adventures—clothes as tough as she was.

Amelia insisted on wearing the first bloomers in town. The townspeople frowned and whispered. Grandmother *tsk-tsked*. She only allowed Amelia to wear bloomers on Saturdays.

Glorious Saturdays! In her bloomers, Amelia could be as boisterous as the boys. She made stilts, scrambled up trees, and climbed onto roofs. Nothing could keep Amelia on the ground, except the most fabulous, splendid . . .

Most of the time, though, Amelia kept her eyes on the skies. When she was a young woman, she moved to California and took her first ride in an airplane.

From the sky, she could see everything. There were swatches of green and brown in the hills below, a river like a ribbon, and then, waves rippling like silk—the ocean!

Amelia didn't want to come down!

Though most pilots were men, Amelia didn't let that stop her. She began taking flying lessons right away. She worked hard to earn money to pay for her training.

In those days, flying was risky—even for experienced pilots. Once, Amelia crash-landed during a lesson, smashing the propeller and landing gear. But she crashed with style, powdering her nose before climbing safely out of the cockpit.

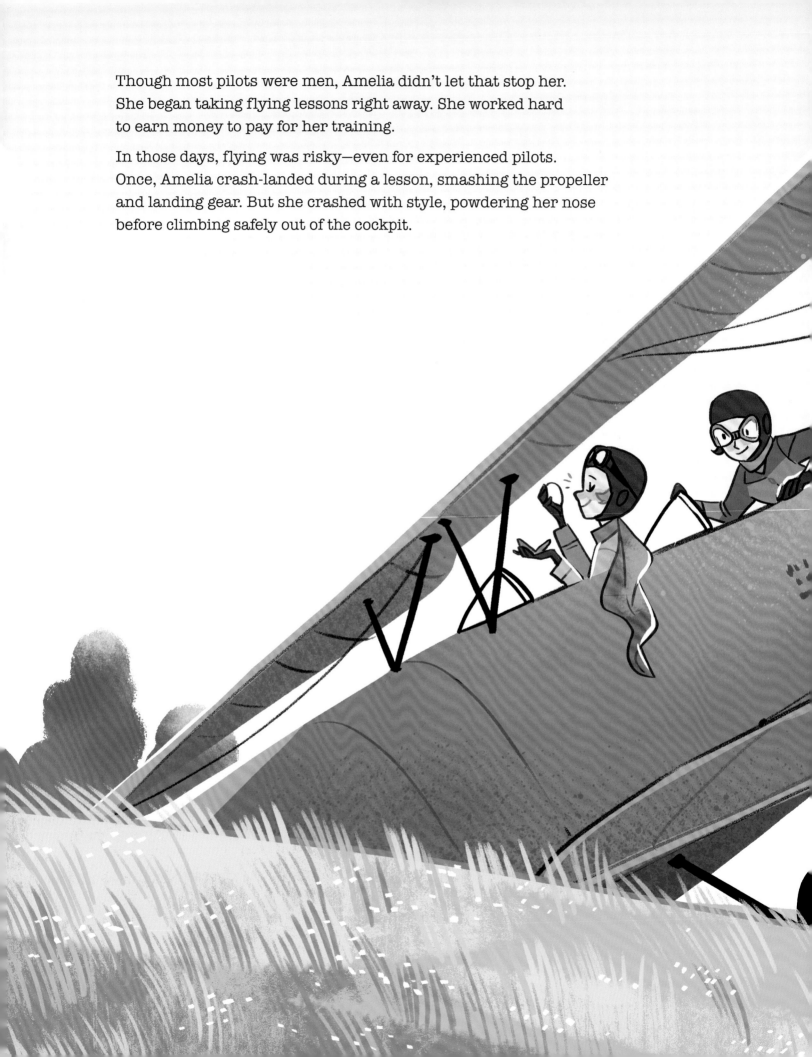

Soon, Amelia learned to thread her plane in and out of the clouds. She flew fast and far, without fear.

"It's so breathtakingly beautiful up there," she said after her first solo flight.

Amelia needed warm, sturdy clothes when she flew. The airfields were dirty. Planes were hard to climb into. And the cockpits were cold.

To fit in with the male pilots, Amelia cut her hair short. She wore trousers and a leather jacket.

Still, Amelia had a way of standing out—by wearing a silk scarf or pearls, and by breaking records.

And soon, when she broke record after record, crowds followed her everywhere.

Amelia liked being famous, except when fans snatched her scarves to keep as souvenirs. People were fascinated by what she did *and* by what she wore. In pilot gear or an evening gown, Amelia shone bright as a star.

Newspapers showed her courage: fearless, daring, and independent.

Fashion magazines showed her style: simple and chic, not frilly or froufrou.

Because flight suits back then were made for men, Amelia designed her own. Her suit had slacks so she could move easily, plus deep pockets for holding pilot logbooks.

But Amelia didn't always dress like a pilot when she flew. In 1933, her good friend First Lady Eleanor Roosevelt invited Amelia to dinner at the White House.

After dinner, Amelia took Eleanor on a night flight. In long gloves and a satin gown, Amelia took a turn at the controls and guided the plane through the starry sky.

As shiny as sequins, the stars seemed close enough to touch.

Back on the ground, Amelia dazzled in fancy frocks created by her friend, Italian designer Elsa Schiaparelli. Amelia told Elsa she wished clothes could be pretty *and* practical. Elsa encouraged Amelia to create just that sort of clothing.

Was Amelia bold enough to launch her very own fashion line? Yes! Especially if it would help her raise more money to pay for her flying adventures!

Amelia set up a design studio in the New York City hotel suite she called home. Using her sewing machine, she dreamed up designs that captured the beauty of flight.

She created fashion for real women, not mannequins . . .

for women of more shapes and sizes,

for women who couldn't sit still,

and even for women who wanted to stand on their heads.

In the 1920s, it wasn't considered ladylike to be active or athletic. But Amelia's designs encouraged women to move freely and be just as active as men.

"I tried to put the freedom that is in flying into the clothes," Amelia explained to a reporter.

And she did! She created twenty-five outfits with zipper pulls shaped like propellers, belts made of parachute cord, and buttons that looked like her plane's wing bolts.

But there was one detail Amelia did not put into her clothes.

"I hate ruffles," she said.

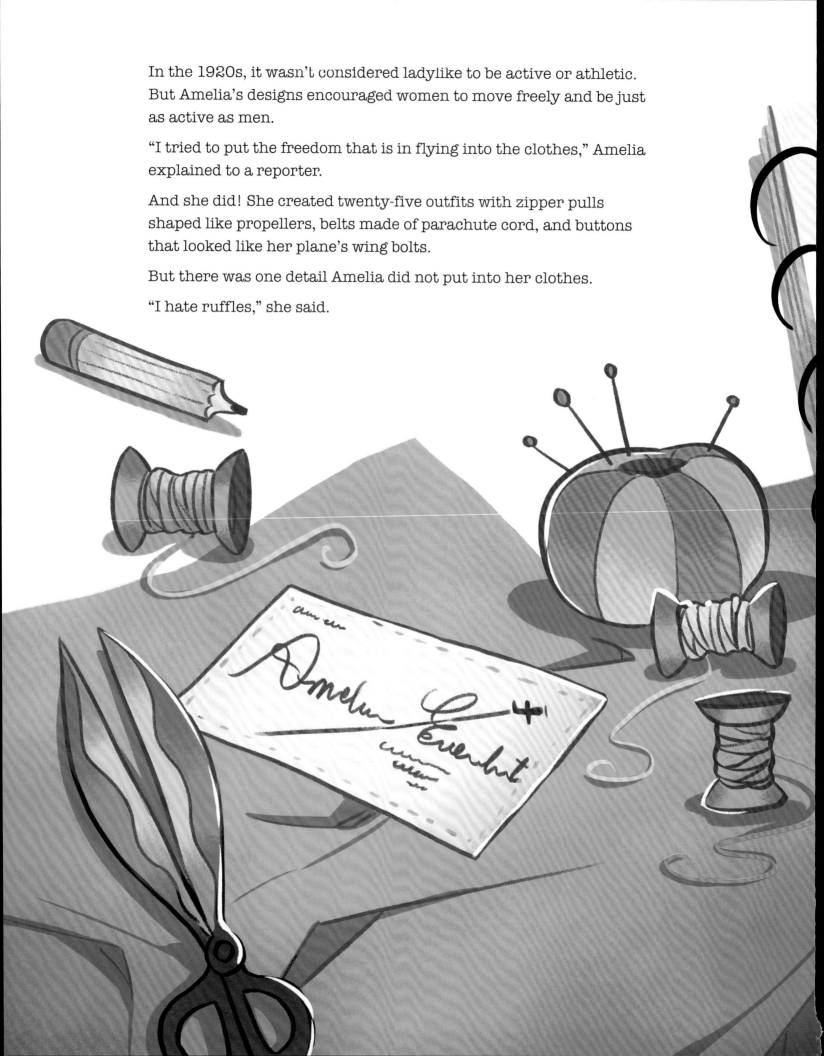

With the launch of Amelia Earhart Fashions, Amelia became America's first celebrity fashion designer.

She used her name and fame to sell her brand in shops across the United States, from New York City to Chicago to San Francisco.

And she modeled the outfits herself.

Girls already loved dressing up like their hero.

Now women could dress like Amelia too.

The small-town girl soared to new heights of stardom
and became one of the most famous people in the world.

First in flight. First in fashion.
Fabulous,
fearless
Amelia!

Author's Note

"Flying is so much more than just a quick way to traverse space.
It's freedom and color and form and style." —Amelia Earhart

As a lifelong Kansan, I grew up hearing about Amelia Earhart. Born in 1897 in Atchison, Kansas, she became one of the world's most famous aviators. Today, it's hard for us to imagine how daring it was for a woman to wear trousers. But Amelia was ahead of her time. She used clothes to defy the expectations and restrictions women—especially women in a male profession—faced in the early twentieth century.

Amelia's fashion collection was an outlet for her creativity. She chose colors, fabrics, and many other details in her collection. Like most modern celebrity fashion designers, she had help from other people, including a seamstress. Her husband, George Putnam, marketed the brand, which sold in thirty cities.

Amelia Earhart Fashions created many innovations that we take for granted today, including:

- shirts long enough to stay tucked in (even if a woman wanted to stretch, bend, or stand on her head!)
- apparel that was comfortable and washable, yet fashionable
- clothes sold as separates rather than a set, so a woman could buy a shirt and a skirt in two different sizes or colors

Although her designs were met with excitement, Amelia Earhart Fashions lasted only one season. In the early 1930s, the United States was in the midst of the Great Depression, so most women couldn't splurge on new clothing. And although the brand helped fund her flying adventures, Amelia felt it took too much time away from actually flying. She declared, "I came to the place where it was either designing or aviation, and I chose aviation."

Even without her own clothing line, Amelia never stopped being a fashion icon. In 1934, the Fashion Designers of America named her one of the ten best-dressed women in America. Amelia even served as an editor for a fashion magazine.

The Kansas state motto is *Ad astra per aspera*—To the stars through difficulties. Amelia exemplified the grace and grit needed to aim for the stars. She showed that a woman could be a skilled pilot and a passionate advocate for women's rights, while at the same time being a fashion trendsetter and entrepreneur.

On her final flight in 1937, Amelia attempted to circle the earth. Sadly, she disappeared over the Pacific Ocean. Her plane has never been found. But to this day, Amelia Earhart remains an American hero and an icon of American style.

Acknowledgments

Special thanks to the following for sharing Amelia Earhart's life with admirers like me:

- Purdue University, Archives & Special Collections, George Palmer Putnam Collection of Amelia Earhart Papers
- Harvard University, Radcliffe Institute, Schlesinger Library, Amelia Earhart Collection
- Smithsonian National Air and Space Museum, Washington, D.C.
- Amelia Earhart Birthplace Museum, Atchison, Kansas
- Atchison County Historical Society Museum, Atchison, Kansas

About the Author

photo credit: Eleanor Wilson

Jennifer Lane Wilson was a lifelong Kansan who grew up learning about the state's hero, Amelia Earhart. Before becoming a children's writer, Jennifer devoted her time to legal writing, parenting, and volunteering. She authored *Soaring in Style* while living with her husband and very fluffy dog in Shawnee, Kansas, a Kansas City suburb. Sadly, Jennifer passed away in 2020 following a battle with breast cancer. Learn more about her life, legacy, and dedication to telling Amelia's story online at jenniferlanewilson.com.

About the Illustrator

photo credit: Lissy Marlin

Lissy Marlin is a *New York Times* best-selling illustrator from the Dominican Republic with a simple mission: bring a little bit of magic to everyday life, one piece of art at a time! In previous years, Lissy played the role of lead artist at a toy company called GoldieBlox, a small start-up dedicated to inspiring the next generation of female engineers. Presently, she spends her days as a freelance illustrator, working from her home in Philadelphia, Pennsylvania.